Peace Behind the Poem

Cover Design By
Reda Washington
Email: washington_rz@yahoo.com

© 2009 by Jonathan Sherman. All rights reserved. ISBN 978-0-578-00832-5

This book is dedicated; to

Murray-Wright High School Class of 2004 and

To all of my friends and family that help contribute to my madness for writing poetry.

Thank You.

Chapter 1: The Dreams   6

Introduction   7
A Dream   7
Dream Girl   8
Nightmare   9
Sleepless   10
Maze   11

Chapter 2: The Love Stories   12

Rose   13
You   13
US   15
The Heart of a Woman   16
Colors of a Dove   17
The Conversation   18
Relationship of Sin   20
The Cheater   21
One Night Stand   22
The Date   23
Confessions of a Sex Freak   26
The one I Love   27
The way I feel for you   28
Helping Hand   29
Helping Hand 2   30
Charlie   31
Break Up: Last Time   31

Chapter 3: The Life   33

What stories are made of?   34

Club Life	35
Millennium	36
Generation X	37
The Stand Off	38
My Life	39
Life in the Eyes of the One	40
The Empty Mind	41
Inside a lonely Man	43

Chapter 4: The End — 45

Welcome Home	46
The Beginning	47
The Dark	47
Devil Nights Hellful Days	48
Walk of Life	49
Drive by	50
Drive by II: The Understanding	51
The World	52
Me II	53

Chapter 5: The Free Mind — 54

Free Write	55
Free Write 11-04-2003	56
Free Write 11-10-2003	58
Free Write 12-09-2003	59
Free Write 01-28-2004	60
Free Write 02-17-2004	61
Free Write 03-30-2004	62
Free Write 10-22-2003	63
Free Write 01-06-2003	64

Chapter 1:
The Dream

Introduction

Times up lights out, my life is at the end of its rope. Time is being wasted, too much pain in the dark. There's no light, no air, no space. The pain is getting closer and closer Death is nearing to the point of existence. As I stare and peer into the dark a light becomes visible but a dark coat comes and then

I…see…. my…maker

The Grim Reaper

A Dream

A man, a street

A friend, a hand

Friendship

Take a walk

To the

Hallway of Doors

To nightmares

That dare to

Share its secrets

To scare you back

To an existence that

Is only known as

The real world

Dream Girl

In the midst of the night
I dream of her
That girl
Only to be interrupted by a noise
That night
I slept
And I dreamed of her
Again I saw her
Clearer
I walked to her hand
Ready
To touch her
Feel her
The dream faded to black
I awoke to the mourning sun
Bright as it was, I hurried to the window
As I Fought the blinds shut and
Back to sleep I tried to go
To find that dream girl of mine
Nothing but darkness and anger
In the heat of the night I dreamt again
I saw her
We talked and walked
Laughed and played
I awoke to an empty
Room as all the nights
Before

Nightmare

Nights I tossed and
Turned
My eyes opened to
An empty room
I awoke out of my
Slumber from a nightmare
Where I was being chased
By a big black cat
Which
Snared and ripped my shirt
Blood running
Down my back
Death was coming
Til
I fell down
Into a black hole
What's next?
Where am I?
Memory's float
Past and I saw
The thing I
Hated the most
Me

Sleepless

I can't sleep
Forcing to stay
Awake
Demons are
Coming for me
Taunting me, haunting my mind
I twist and turn
To fight off the killers
I fight with every bone in my body
I get loose
But I can't win
I try and try
Failing attempts
As I sit thinking
About how I felt
When the nightmare
Became hot and bright
I was in hell

Maze

Trapped in a maze
Of dreams and thoughts
Memories filled the walls
This maze trapped all who entered
I heard cries of people
Who wanted to leave but
Was nowhere to be found
<u>Decisions</u> were to be made
Left or Right
Faith or destiny
Respect or disrespect
Time or money
Anger or happiness
Legal or illegal
Life's current problems
At last I reached the
End of the maze
This big door
Separated me from
The outside world or did
Death choose to change
My fate and a grave
Waited for me on the other side
Was this my destiny?

Chapter 2:

The Love Stories

Rose

The red, white, and yellow
Petals
Fall as the tears fall
On a broken heart
Thorns pierce the
Skin of a broken
Man
To many I cause
Pain and hate
This is the story
Of a broken rose
Of a man

YOU

I walk a fine
Line between heaven and hell
I feel like no other
Still I rise

You bring me joy
Hope, dreams
Possibilities are success
Because of you
Beautiful eyes, soft skin
I lose it every time
I see you
Go crazy when I talk to

You
Fall into a dark essence
When we make love
Uplifted when you're
Around
Down when
You're gone
My heart screams
Your name
I thought it was fatal
When I said
I love you
But
The attraction
Is mutual you love me
As much as I love you
Our love will
Last… last …last
So you guess love is
What we're all about
I love you

Us

You are my star

My world

My motivation

Time is short

So I'll keep it real

Loyalty, trust, and wisdom

We share

Love it or hate it

Alike we are

You may love me now

Hate me later

But our love is everlasting

Touch me I fall

Kiss me I melt

But we stay flawless

In our ways

The Heart of a Woman (years ago)

Time and time
Again
I wait for
My love to come
He has gone to the war
To fight Confederates in
A war against the nation
I mourn, if he was
To come
Back dead
In
A casket of wood
Even if I
Look, wonder, and wish
For his return
If he doesn't
I will be a
Widow at a young age
Forever
To mourn his death
Until my death
I will love him with all
My heart
Til I see him
Again, his name will
Forever live
On upon my heart
Deavan

Colors of a Dove

Black, blue, red is
The words I said
Black is for death because of the
Black roses I
Sent with a blue card filled with
A hateful letter
Kill spelled in red blood
White, black, blue, and silver
White is for your wedding
Dress
Blue is for something old
Something new and
Something true blue
As for Black is the suit I wore
With the top hat and Cane
Silver is for the platinum
I wore on my neck and wrist
Which also you wore
D, which is not added, is for
Diamonds that glitter
And sparkle as you
Walk down the aisle
Pretty as the angels
In heaven
I love you so, so I want
You to be my wife
Just so

You and I
Can say
I do

The Conversion: The Boy's version

Here as we lay on my bed
And kiss
You tell me that
You Love me
And that you're falling in
Love with me

> (I was not looking for this
> Not another relationship
> Not another girl to fall for
> And break my heart like the rest and
> If that wasn't enough I just came out of
> A bad relationship
> Here we go again)

Like I really wanted to say it
For days
But
I can't tell you how I feel about this
It's so strong
More than I had for any boy.

                              (Here she goes
                          Running off at the mouth
                        I brought her here for one reason
                               And that reason was
                                  Only to have sex
                          And she's talking about feelings
                               Where's the way out)

She goes on
I know you might not feel the same way
But I thought
I'd let you know before we
 Go any further---

                               (Stop this sentence
                        I didn't even know we was in a
                                  Relationship
                              Furthermore is this girl
                                      Crazy
                             I need to let her know
                                 That I was just
                                   Trying to hit)

You need to understand how
I feel
Why won't you
Say any thing.

                             (Because I know, it will be
                                  A part two to
                                    This story)

Relationship of sin

From the day, I met you
I guess it was meant to be
But now it seems to me as a
Non-ending dream of problems
That always occurs
I'm mixed in this
Relationship
I feel your cheating
I tried to hide it but
You sensed it in my words
You saw it etched on my
Heart like the
Tattoo on my arm
At some point in time I
Feel like I wanted to die
For the pain of you
Cheating has no forgiveness on
My soul

The Cheater

The heat of the night became
Passion in my bed
This girl that is here is not my
Lover, but a friend
Which make the fire
In the burning eye of mine
I pull her closer I kiss her
Neck
I went inside her bearing walls
With my hat protecting my gun
Push, pull, drag, fall, pain
She screams, shout, and scratch
Blood runs
[Thump] we hit the floor
The heat is intense
She's on top ridin' ridin' and ridin'
The time of night passes
She leaves
Closing her bearing walls
As she leaves, I start to
Dream
Of the passion we had
I awake
And here comes my
Lover

One Night Stand

Dark nights
Lead to
Lonely days

On the couch
By the basement
Stairs
Groans n moans
Twists n pulls
Back n forth
She rocks on my lap
Her thin hips
Apple size
Booty
Onion shaped
Breast
Dark chocolate
Skin
In my mind sex
Is the
Deal
While people
Of the
Night watch

The Date

Slow music plays a romantic
Song than turns to jazz
It plays around and around
I pour the drinks into a
Crystal glass cup that will later
Become a thing of the past
As my eyes would get hazy
There's a knock at the door
My date is here
I said to myself in hopes
Of pleasure in my bed
Dressed in a nice black suit
With my hat tilted to the
Side
I gracefully open the door
Revealing her stunning red Dress
The one I like with the Back out strapless
At that point, I had one Thing in
Mind as she walked in
Looking at her ass tightly wrapped
In her dress like a Christmas gift
We sat and talked for as long as I could
But I can't help her round breast
Hanging all out her dress
As she leans forward
Teasing me
I drool like a dog until the thought
Of her hair swung
Down

I walked towards this Heavenly figure
And gave her a passionate Kiss
It was so intense
I pulled her up and we
Walked slowly to the room
Eyes locked on each other
We took turns each pulling off an article of Clothing
Off of one another
We hit the bed, clothes every where
I looked at this beautiful creature in
Its entirety I reached for a hat for better protection
I slowly entered her secret passage of love
A slow moan came out
She asked for a faster motion
She pulls on the sheets
Grabbing everything in sight
Pulling on my skin trying
To hold back from moaning
Louder
Her inside
So moist and wet as
I thrust in and out
Tainted with her perfume
It smelled like heaven in the making
Her body was as smooth as a petal of
Roses
She whispered in my ear for me to take her there
Make her scream til she was breathless
I slowly incline my speed
Her voice gets louder the room became hotter

She request for faster and harder between each
Moan
I give her what she asks for
A well needed maintenance
I gave in to her every demand til
The end
I cam she cam
And
The night was silent

Confessions of a Sex Freak

Against the wall I'm pinned
She forced me to undress
Pulling on my T-shirt
She has me weak
Brown skin dark eyes the perfect body
I'm surprised
Fierce she was and she
Grabs my dick and massages it
With her tongue til it's hard
I grabbed her quickly spun her around
Snatched her pants down
That pretty, little thong
Tightly gripped to her waist
She fell to the bed
It excited her but
She liked it rough
Without warning
I pulled her body close to mine
And guided myself in
The rush ran through my body
As she screamed my name
Giving it to her long and hard
"Daddy" she says, "Daddy" she screams
I climaxed from the excitement
All in her
I put it
As she climbed down to relax from the mood

> I hopped on the bed and fell asleep
> To wake up to a dream
> Or was it reality

The one who I love

As I lay on this couch
Upon this girls lap
She rubs my chest and smiles
I look into her dark, brown eyes
Then I let her know that
I love her
I let her know that
She is the one
I want to love
She stares
Into my eyes and says
"I love you too, with all my heart and soul"
She then cries and I knew
She was the one

The way I feel for you

A burning feeling
Where a ill
Becomes a
Chill
Still, action takes
Place no movement
Only her
The space where she
Stands turn to black
Red broken hearts
Fills the background
Pain only I can feel
With my knowledge
Of love
This feeling can't be
Be true
But it is
It's –it's
Love

Helping Hand (Girl View)

In the time of need
I call you
But when I hate you
I leave you alone
When I can use you
I take it all
When you're not around
I'm alone, so I miss
You
Its only when I need
You to myself
All to myself
Your mine until
I lose you to another
Girl
Now I'm missing
You
Regretting what I did to you
I don't blame me I blame
You
'Cause it's your fault I'm this way
I can never change
Because I'm just an image of
You
A shadow
And you will be mine
To use and toy with

As long as I live

Helping Hand 2 (Boys View)

To protect and serve
Is what cops do
To kill a man without
Reason is what a thug,
Gangsta and a Killer do
I'm not your servant
Nor
Your pet I have needs
Like any other person
In this world
To ask me to kill on your terms
To please you
You only call
When you need
Me
And any advice that I can
Give you
You find yourself
Trapped
Now your calling and
Calling
But I'm not picking
Up

Charlie

Charlie where are you

Why did you leave?

Where did you go?

It's cold

Dark

I'm alone

Charlie where are you

Charlie its cold

Why did you leave me alone?

I'm sorry

But I'll be

Sorry no more

Just come back to me

I want you back

Charlie I'm sorry

I'm sorry,

Charlie

Break Up: Last Time

Five years down the

Drain

I guess love isn't

Forever

Maybe love is blind I was

Tainted by blood

Over my eyes

To see the game
You played
But in the end
We're both at
Fault
Just give me what
I need I'll leave
Not to say a word
On the phone nor in person
It won't hurt or
Destroy your life
It would only make it better
Five years down the
Drain this time
You know it's
Your fault

Chapter 3:

The Life

What stories are made of?

Come let's talk
In a dark room
Next to the fire
In the soft bedded
Chairs that resemble
Thrones where kings sat
Take a seat let's talk
Of mystical animals
And
Creatures lay sleep
They wait til midnight
Hungry
Come on let's walk
Through graveyards
And
Castles where the walls are cold
And the air is still
Sit on a tombstone on Halloween
And watch the dead arise
Evil faces and skeleton bones
Will awake you from a slumber
To reach out for help
The cold hard ground
To walk again
Come back again
To the dark room where the

Atmosphere

Is uncomfortable but ordinary

Sit by the fire and talk

Of good times past

But keep in mind that the story

I told

It is not all

Of

What it seems

Club Life

Let's talk

Let's walk

In the beginning

It's just an Introduction

Lights down
Darkness appears
The light shines
The music start
Volume up
Bass down
Body moves
Heart jumps
Watch me as I
Tear it up

The rhythm and
Blues
To rap and new soul
Against the wall just a pimp
That can't dance
But the words
Dance out my mouth
To soothe the soul of a
Woman
Till the time is up and

We have to go
Then this playa
Plays this
Game of life
I'm a smooth talkin'
Fast walkin'
Kind of a guy with
Plenty of money on the side
Fast cars, drinks, and women is what my
Club life is about
Watch as I glide and fly
Through the air and move
To the groove
The only thing that can stop
This supafly guy is time
And when the time is up
mourning is
Here
The night was young music
Was hopping
Until next time this is my club life

Millennium

Times of the world
People of a nation
Life of a century
Times has changed
For
The many
This is the new age of people
Let us rise
And embrace
The fore coming
Of men and women
Black and white
Embrace
This new world
Order let us run til' we

Reach
The highest
Mountain and
Embrace it

Generation X

Time, places, and people
Have changed
Kids are
Cursin' as if it was an everyday
Word
Teens
Fourteen and Up
Having babies
What's going on?
Here is a
Nation
Of the new world
Are we
Doomed to a certain destination
Or destruction
Little kids and teens
Dying and
Mothers crying
Now I know why
It's called
Generation X

The Stand Off

As the world turns, I find myself lost in the mind
Of a mad man who is in deep need off help
I have friends who I reach out for
But they're never there
I have a family like most do
That rides my back
And brothers, who break my stuff
Like most people, I live how you would live, if I
Was you, I think like me, but
If I were you, I'd think like you
'Cause I could never be you and you could never be me
So stop judging me and
Try to understand me and
Realize my tragic past
You don't know who I am and
Where I'm from
I stand as a man in front of a
Crowd of haters and say it loud
You didn't make me, I made me
And you will not break my spirit
If you are with me
Then rise to the top of this stage
And say it with me
I am free from the pain of you
And your army of haters
So
Hurt me or break me
But you will

Never be I or understand I
Cause for once in my life
I know who I am

My Life

My life, feel my pain
Look through My eyes
And
See what I see
Come into my Mind and
Know what
I know

Dream my dream
And see me how
I used to be
Write about me
Than be me
But don't
Judge me
Feel my pain
Understand my
Anger

Hear me roar, yell
Shout to the highest mountain and the deepest valley
Blue water

Dark skies flood
The inside of
My mind
I'm blind to the
Believer and to the
Rest of society

I know love when
I feel it
Can you see it in me?
Do you know me?
NO
Then don't judge me
I can show love
But
Can't express it
I know whom I love
But that love has been lost
You know who she is loud and a Gemini
If you know
You know
Don't judge her

On her actions
If you don't know her
Don't judge her
Judge me
For this is
My…life…A
Thug's life…a friend's life…a lover's life
This… is…my
Life
Until the End

Life in the Eyes of the One

Life in this world is a sin
People don't understand
How we are the last of our existence
The last of our people, of our generation

Kill, Murder, Death
Is what we see in the
World today
War against our own
This is the Society of our
Black people
Start the new revelation, the new nation
Begin the annihilation and reconstruction of our country
From the bottom up

To the women don't be discouraged
To the men that hit on you
Get away to a better life
Find the power to
Get up and depart the place where sins
Are the only thing that exist in your life

Find a new life where you can live in peace
And have children
Don't live in the blue and
Lie in the dark for life

The Empty Mind

I await in the dark corners
Waiting patiently
Unaware of this feeling
Stirring in my heart
My stomach filled
With vodka and
Gin
Drunk with disgust
Sick cause of not
Eatin'
Mind blurred of
Images
That can't be understood
Why must it end this way?
Trapped inside my own mind

Fighting my guilt
Swallowing my pride
Burning my courage
Scared of fear
Living in darkness
What it takes to write this
Is the darkness within my heart?
 It conquered the outer most regions
Of the mind
It is
Deavan the Reaper
So I burn inside
Of my own
Mind
When my clock stops
And the end is near
I'll be free
Til' then I'm a prisoner at
Heart
There's only one key
Love

Inside a lonely man

I sit back in my room

Pitch black peering into the

Dark

Watch the sun light

Pass by the creaks in the

Wall

Birds by the window

Darkness in my head

Like an open book

You can read my thoughts

And dreams

Open a door see daylight

Open my mind see darkness

The evil in the eye of

The lord passed a curse

Upon me of sad days and

Evil nights

No happiness exist here

Bad dreams and nightmares appear

On the distant wall

Friends are allies, foes, as well as enemies

Death to the hated

Riches to the liked

I mean what I say

Don't understand what I'm doin'

why so mad?

Don't know, don't care

Where's the concern?

Where's the love?

Stop the hate, the madness

I stop my hate and let

The tears fall

I cried all night

Til' the sun

Dried my tears

Why did

I cry from the hurt

Pain that pass through me

The years fly like

A bird flies

Let it all go

Open your mind

Express yourself, your feelings

Get smart get better

Stay from trouble

Be honest stay true be

Loved

Love someone

And then you can open

Your mind and hear me

Chapter 4:

The End

Welcome Home: Rain City

Lets walk into the mind of a
Mad man
Walk into the world of a killer
Take a step in a conquers shoes
To take over the
World
I'd like to take you to Rain City
A world of family feuds, world gossip, and
Death
Tales of sadness
You're never welcome when you
Come here or
Invited
This place exist only in
A place that haunts your mind
The inner anger that
Holds you down and the
People who gets you in
The mood to die
Watch as life turns
And hell burns 'cause the
Only way out of Rain City
Is death
Welcome Home!!!

The Beginning

The road ends
Here
A new life begins
There
We have to go
There
To find
The new
Life
That waits
Us
On the other
Side

The Dark

The light is close, I can't move to the light.

(Dark voice: Death is waiting now come to the dark side)

The voice is near, I can move, and I run but before I knew it

Death…is …I

Devil Nights, Hellful days

Day and night
I step out
The dark shadows
To embrace upon
Life its existence
What am I to do?

Day	Night
People are	Dreams take flight
Annoying me	Dark clouds feel the
What do people want from	Mind
Me	The sky turns
What can I give them?	Thunder, lighting, and nightmares
But	Feel the room
When the days out	Then
Night falls	Night turns day

Walk of Life

I walk the path of a
                Corpse
Dead in the streets when you
                See me
You see nothing but
                Bones
They have a warrant out for my
                Arrest
While others want to put me to
                Rest
On my back six feet deep
                Under the ground
Fully equipped with a
                Gun
To fire and murder innocent
                Victims
At my own will
                What
My future holds for me
                Nothing
But a bloody shirt a
                Baby
Four gun wounds
                Life
Three felonies two deaths
                And

One funeral
        Mine

Drive by

Nine to five

You can stay

Alive

Ten to three

Is where your hands

Are to be

When you see a car at three o'clock

With the

Headlights off, hands at

Twelve

Guns at one

You run 'cause

The only thing you hear

Is

Drive by

Drive by II: The Understanding

You sit on your porch knowing the game

Are you smart or a fool for the star struck disaster?

Alone in the world you can't see the people

Who thought they knew you

They didn't.

You see the car

Up the block

Your gun is held in your hand

A gun in there hand

Who will win?

Five deep in an Escalade

Lights turned low

Music turned down

Silence

You hear your heart beat

Off every breath you take

You grip the gun

Your eyelids come down

Then up

You wait

For their move

They slowly creep up the street

You take the gun off safety

They drive faster and

Now in range

The guns blast your way

You duck and dodge them the best you can

You blast back as you run and get one in the leg

They still shooting
They see you down
You still shoot back blast for blast and
On your last clip
You run out
The battle was short
You drop the gun and run to
The alley for safety
They pull off and the fight is
Over
You live to see another day

In my world, there is a winner and a loser and just so you know, the winner, dies just like the loser. As my brother always told me, you can't win for losing.

The World

Bent on revenge
Hatred against your
Kind
Who can judge you?
Unlike how you hate me
Am I the reason for threats upon society?
The last of a generation
Or the new death in the
World
How close to the end are we?
So close that life passes
Us by

ME II

After me
There will be none
Before me
There was many
I am the last
Until it's done

Chapter 5:

Free Mind

Free Write

When is enough an enough?
When you drink and drive
Your life goes by
Drowning in your sorrow
Of your tears and pity
A field of memories
Plagues the mind
And sweetens the
Taste of the infamous
Alcohol
As you stare into the
Bottom of the bottle
How hollow a glass can be?
Lonely
As you
See the times
That past of
A drunken habit
That progress
And involves into
The demon within

Free Write 11-04-03

Temptation is hard
Life or death
What will you choose?

Death

In the darkness
Where evil lies
Hides demons and
Devils
Sprits of Dead
Soldiers
Graves and
Tombstones that
Hide the very
Secret that is
Known to man
Walk along the
Path of a
Foolish Man
With nothing
To live for and
Everything to lose
Run to your house
'Cause in a world
Of death evil has
No boundaries desperately
You run and try to

Hide but no one
Can save you now
'Cause once evil
Always evil

Life

In the life
Walk a path
Of righteousness
And be good
And help others
Beware for those
Who try to take advantage and
Control of your good heart
Be a good man
And loyal friend
This will
Prevent and keep
Evil at bay by
The push of your
Hand
No! So watch your back
Choose your friends wisely
And
Don't get
Beat down
To the dirt
                        Which will you choose?
                        Pick your path wisely, death or life

Free Write 11-10-03

Destination is key

Movement is knowledge

Watch as I rise to the

Top to overcome the physical

Boundaries

Walk the line down the

Road til' it's a fork

And a decision has

To be made

Let your spirit guide you

Watch you back

For left and right

Equal right and wrong

Life or death, live or die

Can you survive?

The dark road of danger

The oozing slime off

The trees makes the

Ground squishy under your

Feet with each step

You sink deeper and

Deeper

You're getting stuck at every turn

What do you do?

Free Write 12-09-03

I'm tired of the endless
Days and nights
Boredom easily sits in
To check into my life
I, asleep, awake
In a rush of a
Dream not yet to
Pass
For whatever reason
To my understanding I'm
Admired until I'm awake
Meaning I had a bad
Dream
Of which I can't recall
Not a demon or new car
In my mind
But a new image
Or rip in time
To see what could
Or can be
Of only
One person
Me

Free Write 01-28-04

In a vast nation
Of enemies
I stand-alone
In a building at
The bottom trying to
Make it to the top
Walk with me through
This epic journey to the high rise
Of this tower
Foes with unlimited
Ability trying to conquer what is mine
This tower
I have to gather all
My greatest abilities
To reach and grab
What I desire most
Is my life long dream
To succeed
Even with all the odds in
Their favor
I have to be
Me
I have to succeed
'Cause no one
Or
No man will
Hold me down
(Gun cock)

Free Write 02-17-04

Walk to the end
And tell me
What you see
A future
Or
A dead end
Touch the world
And make
A Difference to
Change a life
Or bring a new life
To this world
And watch it grow
To become the
Very same future
That you have
Become

Free Write 03-30-04

Dark dim lights
I drive down a weary road
For hours I drove
Down that road through
The pitch-black fog
Around and around
I'm exhausted from this
Long ride to the countryside
As I doze off at the
Wheel it turns left
I suddenly jump up
And grab the wheel
I drive wildly over the road
For control until
A deer enters the road
As I crash just barely
Missing
The deer
Unconscious I am
As I lay, back in the car and take in
Every last breathe I
Have left

Free Write 10-22-03

Walk, talk, and breathe

Life into your

Existing body

Deep down

Inside past

Your lungs

Deeper you go

Past the stomach and

Around the Intestines

Into the part

Of your body

Dark and dirty

Damper with

Cells and breathless air

In the corner

Of the body

Is where I lay

And sleep

Where I find peace

It's in this dark

Dirty walls of your body

Watching cells go by

Filling guts with air

And I stare

Wondering

What will tomorrow bring

Free Write 01-06-03

Walk the mile that

A man with no soul

Bares

The dark that engulfs

The flames

And burns the water up in smoke

Dark places in

My mind

Empty

Echoes stretch across

The walls

Deep down past

Thoughts and memories

To a new person

That takes hold

The evil in me

Now surfaces

Not the devil

A power unlike any evil

He prefers to be called

Deavan

"I lived in darkness for years
And through
My writing I have found
Peace behind the Poem"